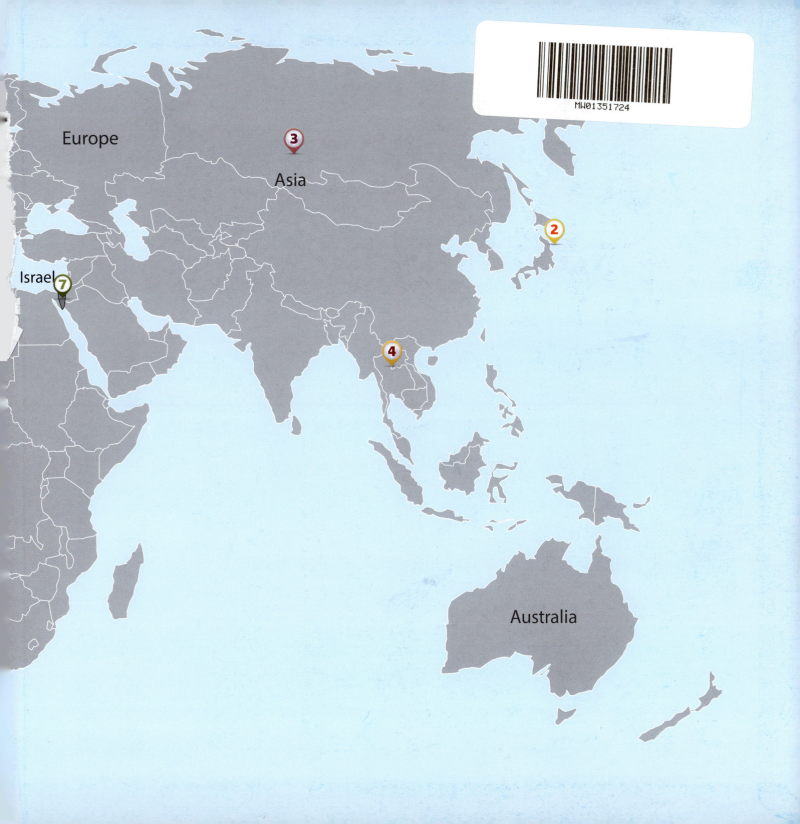

Translated by: Sashi Fridman

Content Editor: Yael Mermelstein

Copyright © Ella Verzov • Chana Oirechman

All rights reserved. No part or picture of this book may be reproduced, translated, photographed, stored in a retrieval system or transmitted in any form or by any means, without written permission from the authors.
www.younglamplighters.com | yeladim.e.c@gmail.com.

Photography: Vinicio Tassani

Layout and Design: Boaz Sharon

Photo Editing: Yanki Schechter

Special thanks to Tamar Rieber and family

Published by Menucha Publishers Inc.
250 44th Street, Brooklyn, NY 11232
Tel/Fax: 718-232-0856
1855-Menucha | www.menuchapublishers.com
ISBN - 978161465170-3

ב"ה

Tamar of Venice

Young Lamplighters

By **Ella Verzov** • **Chana Oirechman**
Translated by **Sashi Fridman**

Hi! My name is Tamar. I'm seven years old but my mother likes to say that I'm seven years young. I live in Italy in an amazing city called Venice. If you want to know how to pronounce the word Venice, it rhymes with the word tennis!

Do you ever wake up with an exciting feeling, but you can't remember why you're excited? That's what happens to me when I wake up this morning. I'm not sure why I wake up with such a good feeling. But then I remember – it's Wednesday! Wednesday is my second favorite day of the week. Very soon, you'll understand why it's my second favorite day of the week. Guess what my favorite day is?

I say *Modeh Ani*, the morning prayer, thanking G-d for a brand-new day. The sun is shining and there's a delicious smell coming from the kitchen. I wash my hands. Then I close my eyes and smile. It smells like it's going to be a great day!

My street

When I open my eyes I see my special certificate hanging on the wall. Which special certificate? Well, the day that we set off to live in Venice as messengers of the Lubavitcher Rebbe, my mother found a large envelope in her mailbox – with my name on it! The envelope held a certificate letting me know that a letter was bought for me in a Torah scroll written in honor of Jewish children. I was only two months old at the time and I already had a letter written in my honor in a *sefer Torah*! Did you ever get mail before you could read?

My letter in the Torah happened to be from *Lech Lecha* – a portion in the first book of the Torah, the book of *Bereishit*, Genesis. That's the portion where G-d tells Abraham to leave his homeland and he does. We were about to do exactly the same thing!

"This is definitely a blessing from G-d for a successful trip," my parents said. They packed the certificate in a special place inside our suitcases. When we arrived in Venice, they hung it on the wall opposite my bed. When I look at it every morning, it makes me feel special and it reminds me of why I'm here in Venice.

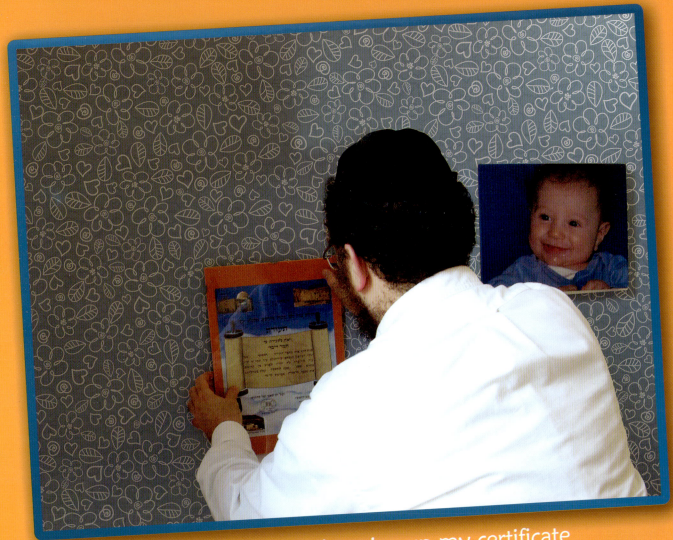

My father hanging up my certificate

As I get ready to leave for school I look out the window and what do I see? I don't see trees or flowers or cars. I don't see people walking their dogs because if I saw that, the dogs and the people would have to be swimming! That's because all I see outside my window is water, water, water everywhere.

You see, our house is a three-story orange building which is located between two canals of water. On one side of our house there's also a sidewalk where people can walk, and on the other side there's water flowing right under my window! If I drop anything out of my window I'd have to put on goggles and go diving to find it!

But I can't spend too much time at my window. School is starting soon. I have to run!

The canal of water near my house

You'll never guess how I get to school in the morning. I don't go by yellow school bus. I don't go by car. I go by boat!

Venice is a city on water. In our city there are no roads and no cars. Instead of roads there are canals of water with sidewalks alongside them where people can walk. We get around by either walking or taking a bus – but not the kind of bus that you're familiar with. In Venice the bus is a boat (it's called a *vaporetto* in Italian) and it sails down the canals. The water bus has a driver and you need to buy a ticket to travel on it just as you would on an ordinary bus. In the morning, our *vaporetto* is packed with people heading to work and with tourists who come to visit our unusual city built on water.

The water bus travels around Venice and stops at different stations. The stations are floating planks of wood that are tied to the sidewalk. While waiting for the *vaporetto* we can feel the station shaking underneath our feet from the waves that flow under them. Can you imagine your bus stop shaking under your feet? You'd run for help!

The main street in Venice

The water bus arrives

The *vaporetto* sails around the city of Venice, but not in the canals that cross the city. Those canals are too narrow. The bridges over them are so low that you can bump your head on them if you stand up. Make sure to duck! The *vaporetto* uses the wide canals surrounding the city.

Visitors to Venice enjoy riding in gondolas, which are very narrow, long boats that are small enough to sail down the canals and under the bridges. Small motor boats are also used in the canals. There are taxi boats, ambulance boats, and even cargo boats which are like trucks on water.

Most people in Venice have their own private boat which they dock in the canal near their homes. The boat is like the family car, without seat belts! The water is like a driveway!

A gondola passing under the bridge

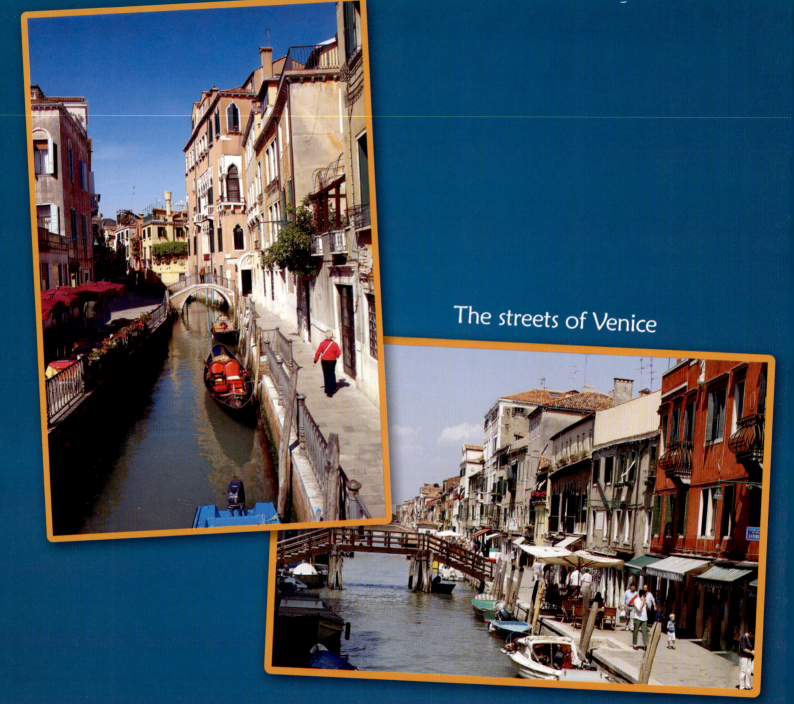

The streets of Venice

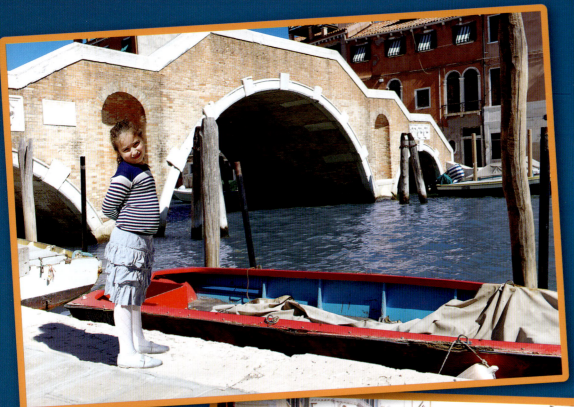

I can walk to school if I want to. It only takes ten minutes. But tell me, if you could walk to school or *sail* to school, which one would you choose? I choose sailing. I stand on the deck, the wind blowing through my hair and the deep blue waters rushing all around me…

On deck on the way to school

Can you imagine looking forward to your ride to school?

I like going to school almost as much as I like getting there. There's only one Jewish school in Venice. I'm in second grade. Guess how many kids there are in my class besides me?

One!

My friend Chana is the only other girl in my class. Can you guess who my best friend is? Chana!

Her father is the head *shaliach*, messenger, in our city. We always sit near each other and play together at recess. If we play games we don't even have to pick teams!

If I'm absent, half the class is empty. It makes me feel kind of important. And I love my teacher. She came from Israel just to teach us. All of our schoolbooks come from Israel, too.

Preparing homework

As much as I love sailing to and from school, today I must walk home. Why? Because it's Wednesday! On Wednesdays I walk home across two bridges and two canals. I'm careful to stay away from the canal because there are no guardrails or gates between the sidewalks and the canals. Even my two-year-old little brother knows to be careful not to get too close to the canals.

Some days, an interesting thing happens. Even when I walk home, I walk in water. Really! Let me explain.

On my way home

A few times a year, the sea level rises. That means the water gets higher and higher and higher until – whoosh! The canals overflow into the streets of Venice. There are some streets that get so flooded that you can't even walk there. Other streets can be walked on as long as you're wearing high rubber boots. My brother and I have these boots. On days that the sidewalks are flooded, we can't leave the house without them. That's because the water can get really high – over my knees! When the water is even higher than our boots we can't even go outside. We just have to wait inside until the water level goes down.

Does that sound like fun? Truthfully, I prefer to splash in small puddles with my boots instead of trying to walk through a flood.

The flooded city

And now, it's finally time to tell you about – Wednesday! My second most favorite day of the week. Wednesday after school is shopping day. On the way home my mother takes me to a special fish market called *Pescheria*. I know how to find kosher fish, the ones with fins and scales. I'm so used to the smell of fish that I don't even need to pinch my nose. We go fishing for Shabbat at the fish market! The salesman wraps up the fish that we buy in special paper and we carry them home in special baskets.

As I get closer to home, we pass by Carlos's fruit and vegetable stand. He's known me since I was a baby and he always treats me to a juicy fruit when I pass by.

A fresh fish straight from the sea

At Carlos's fruit and vegetable stand

Back at home I have lunch and I do my homework. I love playing with friends. When Chana comes over, we play with dolls or tic-tac-toe or other fun games.

I have two other good friends but I only see them a few times a year. They live far away in the city of Milan. I have to travel two and a half hours by train if I want to see them. Sometimes I visit them and sometimes they come to visit me.

I actually have other friends in Venice, too. Every girl who comes to my house becomes my friend. That's why I'm here. I'm here for all the young Jewish girls in Venice. I try my best to be nice to all my guests – even when they want to use my favorite toys. I want to be a good example of someone who keeps the Torah commandments.

Playing with Yuvali

After lunch I also have chores to do at home. I help with my three little brothers, Memi, Tzvi and Shlomik. They're the cutest little brothers in the whole world. If you have little brothers, though, you might not agree with me. I love to read them books. I also like folding laundry. I like watching how my mother stacks neatly folded clothing back in the closet. The clothing looks like soldiers.

My sweet brothers listening as I read them a story

Later, I put on my pink and black rollerblades and I go out rollerblading with my brothers. Sometimes my mother or my father comes with us. We love zooming down the narrow streets of Venice. But, boy, do we have to be careful – there are canals at the end of every street. Look out!

We live in the Jewish ghetto in Venice. This is the area that is the center of Jewish religious life in Venice. Many years ago, Jews were forced to live here, and that's why it's called a ghetto. Today, we choose to live here. Our Chabad House is here, right in the middle of the ghetto square. Jews from all over the world can come into the Chabad House to put on *tefillin*, give *tzedakah* and lots of other important things!

Memi, Tzvi and me, rollerblading along the canal

Right near the Chabad House there's a yeshivah – a Jewish school for boys. Boys from all over the world come to study in the yeshivah. My father is the head of the yeshivah. I love peeking through the window to watch him learning with the students there. He's also the rabbi of the synagogue. And he teaches Torah classes to the Jews living in Venice. My father does so many things. But he doesn't run a supermarket! And today is shopping day. We still have more shopping to do!

I like watching my father teach

Our whole family takes the *vaporetto* to the train station. From there we take the train to the nearby city of Mestre. In Mestre there are regular streets with cars and buses. There is also a big supermarket (in Italian we say *supermercato*). That's where we do all of our shopping for Shabbat.

I love shopping in this giant store. I like helping my parents load the shopping cart, filling up the bags with groceries and paying the cashier.

The way home isn't easy. We don't have a car to take home our groceries. We have to carry our heavy bags all the way to the station and then load them onto the water bus. I try to help by carrying one or two bags. By the time we get home, the moon and the stars are already starting to shine.

On my way to shop with my father and Tzvi

I'm tired, but happy. Before I go to sleep, my mother and I plan which foods we're going to prepare for Shabbat.

Baking for Shabbat is one of my regular chores at home. I love helping my mother bake the challah (traditional braided loaves of bread). My mother taught me how to braid six strands of dough! The dough is soft as a pillow.

I also help to prepare desserts. I usually suggest which dessert we're going to make. So, what would you like for Shabbat? Jello? Cake? Fruit salad? I prepare it with my mother and taste it to make sure it came out yummy. Tasting is the most important part!

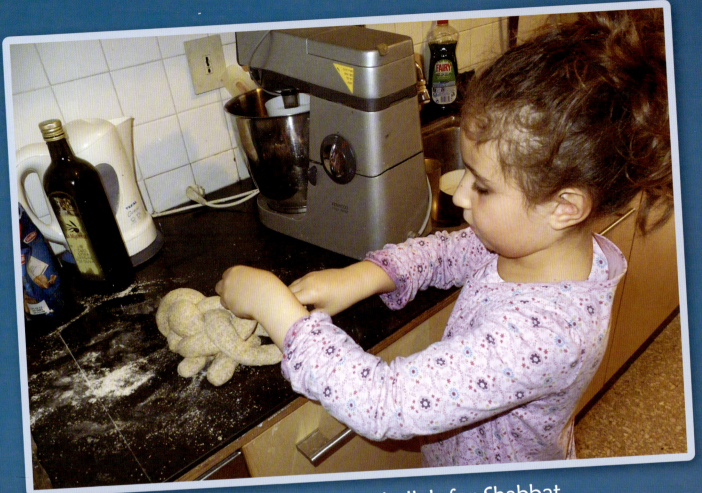
Braiding challah for Shabbat

We always have lots of guests for Shabbat; Jewish families from our city, yeshivah students, and lots of tourists. Every Friday I set two tables; one for the guests and another smaller table for the children. We always have children who come to be our Shabbat guests as well. I'm in charge of the children's table. I told you I have lots of friends in Venice!

Friday night we stay up until very late talking and singing. I get so tired that after I recite Grace after Meals I go to my room and fall asleep while everyone is still singing. I love listening to all the different songs that our guests bring along with them from all over the world.

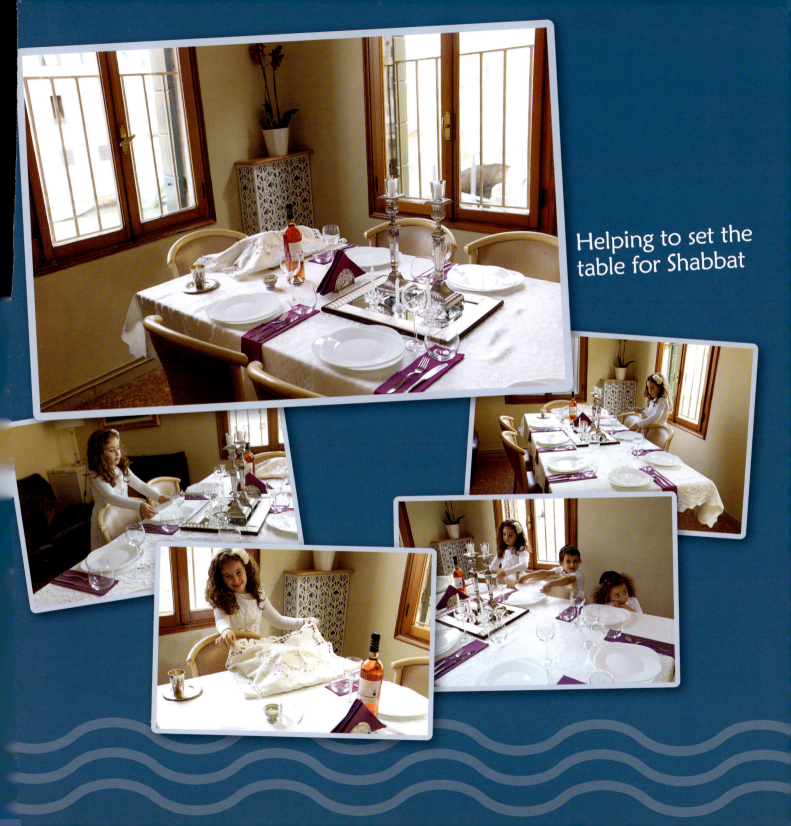

Helping to set the table for Shabbat

Sometimes we join the Friday night Shabbat meal in the kosher restaurant at the entrance to the ghetto. All tourists in Venice are invited to that meal. Sometimes tourists plan to come for Shabbat just so they can eat in the restaurant! It's exciting to see the oldest Jewish ghetto in the world bursting with Jewish life again.

At the entrance to the ancient Jewish ghetto

On Shabbat mornings, everyone prays in the synagogue. The children have their own special room where the yeshivah students pray with them. I try to help girls pray by showing them which prayers to say and when.

In front of the old synagogue in the Jewish ghetto

Thinking about Shabbat, I realize I don't want to be tired tomorrow! I'd better go to sleep. I close my eyes and I count challah rolls lined up in rows to help me fall asleep. I say *Shema*, the prayer before going to sleep, and I get ready for bed. I look out my window at the canal. The lights are on and it looks so peaceful. But I can't help thinking about my past summer vacation when I visited Israel. I remember meeting my grandparents and my cousins. I had so many friends and relatives!

I like living in Venice, but I'll let you in on a little secret: I miss Israel. Sometimes I wish I could just board the water bus and sail off to Israel whenever I feel like it…

Looking out my window and remembering…

But then I close my eyes and I remember all the good things about Venice. I think of all the Jews we're here for. I think of the canals and my boots and my rollerblades. I think about the fish market and Carlos the fruit and vegetable man who always asks how my brothers are doing. I think about all of the people that come to our Shabbat table. I think about all of the people we are bringing close to Torah. I know that very soon, with the coming of Moshiach, we will all be together in Jerusalem, in the Holy Land.

I close my eyes and think of the good things I do in Venice

Now how like that?
Fascinating facts about Venice

Venice is built on 117 small islands. There are 150 canals and 409 bridges in Venice.

When temperatures drop too low in the winter, the canals freeze and boats are unable to travel.

Thirteen million tourists visit Venice each year.

The main canal in Venice is called the Grand Canal. It winds through the city in the shape of the letter S and is graced by beautiful palaces on either side where nobles once lived.

All of the merchandise sold in Venice's shops is brought in via boats.

do you

The Rialto Bridge was the first bridge built over the Grand Canal five hundred years ago. The area of the bridge is Venice's industrial center and is filled with tourists at all hours of the day.

Venice can be reached by boat or by a train that runs on a long bridge built over the water.

The *vaporetto*, or water bus, does not sail on two separate routes going and coming. It sails in a circle around Venice and stops alternately on each side of the canal, stopping on the right and then on the left, right, left, and so on.

Venice is famous for its glassmaking. Many artisans who create beautiful glass works can be found along Venice's alleys. The center for glassmaking is located on the Venetian island of Murano, off the shore of Venice.

Venice often experiences an unusual phenomenon called *acqua alta* (high water). Several times a year, when the sea level rises, the water in the canals overflows and floods the streets of Venice.

The city is prepared for these floods and was built accordingly. There are special grooves in the streets through which the waters burst forth, thereby preventing water from accumulating under the pavement and cobblestones and causing them to be dislodged.

When the water level is very high a siren is sounded throughout the city. In the center of the flooded streets there are elevated platforms for pedestrians to walk on. Venice's residents wear very high boots that reach their thighs so that they can walk in the water without getting wet. When there is very severe flooding, the water level in the canals is so high that boats are unable to pass underneath the bridges and so there is no sailing at such times.

Venice has a magnificent Jewish past. As far back as 1500 years ago, there existed a small Jewish community in the city. The Jewish community at that time was comprised of Jews who arrived from Israel, Turkey, Germany and other parts of Italy. The community of Venice grew after the Spanish expulsion when many Jewish refugees settled in Venice.

Many years ago, Jews were forbidden from settling wherever they wished and were forced to live in the ghetto quarter. This quarter was called the ghetto because it contained a foundry which in the Venetian dialect was called *gheto*. The ghetto in Venice is the oldest ghetto in the world and is the source for the word ghetto, which refers to specific areas where Jews lived in great concentration.

The Jewish community of Venice today is made up of 540 members who live mostly throughout the city, not in the ghetto.

There are five ancient synagogues in the city, two of which are still functional.

The Chabad House, kosher restaurant, synagogue, and yeshivah are located within the ghetto.

The Chabad House of Venice has been functioning for over twenty years. Among its many services, the Chabad House holds prayers three times a day and offers regular Torah classes to members of the community. There is also an institute for rabbinic ordination, a women's club, a school, and a summer camp. Chabad also organizes *chuppah*, bar mitzvah and *brit milah* celebrations. The restaurant and kosher pizza shops are also projects of Chabad of Venice.

IN ITALIAN WE SAY:

Hello – ciao

How are you – come stai

Please – per favore

Thanks – grazie

Mommy – Mamma

Daddy – Papa

Boy – bambino

Girl – bambina

Friend (male) – amico

Friend (female) – amica

Game – gioco

Book – libro

Car - auto

Other books in the Young Lamplighters series

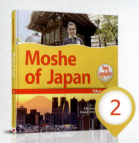 

Moshe of Japan: Eight-year-old Moshe was born in Japan. He studies in a virtual classroom with students from all over the world. His best friend lives in China, a five-hour plane ride away. **Come travel with Moshe, the young lamplighter in the city of Tokyo, the capital of Japan.**

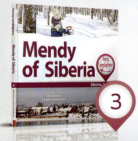 

Mendy of Siberia: Five-year-old Mendy lives in Siberia. The Siberian winter lasts more than half the year. Mendy loves sledding on the snow, touring a city built entirely of ice, and helping his parents to prepare for the Chanukah holiday. **Come travel with Mendy, the young lamplighter in the city of Krasnoyarsk, in frozen Siberia.**

Rivka of Thailand: Eight-year-old Rivka lives in Bangkok, the capital of Thailand. Rivka enjoys visiting the floating market, drinking coconut milk straight from the shell, and watching Lampung the chef dice vegetables into a huge frying pan. **Come travel with Rivka, the young lamplighter in the Far East, in the tropical country of Thailand.**

Explore the world with the Young Lamplighters